Getting Ahead at Work

Carol Staudacher

and

Susan M. Freese

LIFESKILLS™ **HANDBOOKS**

21st CENTURY

SADDLEBACK
EDUCATIONAL PUBLISHING

SADDLEBACK
EDUCATIONAL PUBLISHING
www.sdlback.com

ISBN-13: 978-1-61651-692-5
ISBN-10: 1-61651-692-5
eBook: 978-1-61247-344-4

Printed in Guangzhou, China
1111/CA21101811

16 15 14 13 12   1 2 3 4 5

Contents

Off to a Good Start

Starting a new job can be both exciting and scary. You want to do good work, and you want to get along well with your co-workers. But you have lots of questions! You'll find answers to some of those questions in the employee handbook. And you'll figure out other things on your own if you follow some basic guidelines for starting a new job.

The First Two Weeks

Katie couldn't believe how quickly the past two weeks had gone by! That's how long she'd been at her new job. She was working as an administrative assistant at an accounting firm. And all in all, things were going pretty well.

Looking back, Katie thought about her first day. She'd filled out a lot of forms to sign up for health insurance and other benefits. She'd also been given a copy of the employee handbook. Her supervisor had told her to read through it. It contained information about everything from paid vacation time to what employees were expected to wear.

During the first week, Katie had met all of the people in the office. She'd been a little nervous, but she didn't think her co-workers had noticed. She'd shaken hands confidently with each person. Since then, she'd worked with several

of them. Everyone had been great about training her and answering all her questions.

At the end of Katie's first week, two of her co-workers, Morgan and Lucy, had invited her to lunch. That had really made her feel welcome! But at the lunch, she'd learned much more about Lucy's personal life than she wanted to know. And since then, Lucy had been stopping by her desk to chat. All this made Katie uncomfortable. She wasn't sure what to do.

But today, at the end of her second week, Katie had no worries. She'd received her first paycheck! Katie looked forward to many more weeks at her new job.

nings Information	Current		M /02
mal Gross	4,389.30		
uctions	0.00		
itions	0.00	Year to Date	
rtime	0.00		
EARNINGS TOTAL	4,389.30	5,277.30	
	351.14	418.18	
-Taxable Gross	3,971.12	4,859.12	
able Gross			

atutory & Other Deductions	Current	Year to Date
leral Withholding	311.17	311.17
litional Federal Withholding	0.00	*****
ate Withholding	135.96	135.96
litional State Withholding	0.00	*****
SDI	0.00	55.06
licare	62.67	75.55
licare Buyout	0.00	0.00
ate Disability Insurance	0.00	0.00
RS	351.14	351.14
RS	0.00	0.00
rnate Retirement	67.04	0.00

CHAPTER **1**

The Importance of First Impressions

When we meet someone for the first time, we get a quick idea of what he or she is like. The opinion we form is called a first *impression*. Usually, a first impression is formed within the first few minutes of meeting someone.

When you start a new job, your co-workers will judge you quickly. For that reason, it's important to think about the image you present. Do what you can to make sure the image you present is a good one.

Impression

A general feeling or belief. The *impression* you make on someone is what he or she remembers most about you.

Tips for Making a Good First Impression

- **Don't be late.** On your first day, arrive a few minutes early. You don't want to keep anyone waiting.

- **Look good.** Your appearance is the first thing people notice. Make sure you're well dressed and well groomed.

- **Smile!** Flashing a simple smile will help put everyone in a good mood.

- **Be polite.** Show that you're interested in what others have to say. And when you meet someone, use his or her name in the conversation. Doing so will help you remember names.

- **Be yourself.** Don't try to impress people by being overly friendly or acting like you know more than you do. Have confidence in who you are.

Making a Good First Impression

1. **Wear clothing that's appropriate for the workplace.** If your clothes are too fancy or formal, it will seem like you're trying to attract attention. If your clothes are too casual or informal, it might seem that your work isn't important. And of course, it's never *appropriate* to wear clothes that are revealing—for instance, tight pants or a blouse with a low neckline. Choose basic, everyday clothes, such as a neat blouse or shirt and a nice pair of pants. If you're not sure what to wear, pay

> **Appropriate**
> Proper or correct for the situation.

attention to what most of your co-workers wear. Also remember that in most cases, it's better to be dressed too formally than too casually.

Know the Dress Code

Most companies have a *dress code*. It tells employees what kinds of clothes they're expected to wear.

In many workplaces, the dress code is what's called *business casual*. Business casual allows you to look professional but be comfortable. Don't take comfort too far, though. What you wear to a sporting event or when going out with friends isn't usually appropriate for the workplace. And it's never appropriate to where clothing that's wrinkled, torn, or dirty. Keep in mind that your appearance on the job says a lot about your attitude toward your work.

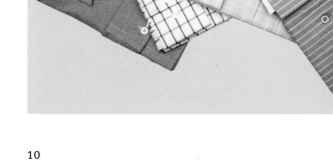

Tips for the Perfect Handshake

A person's handshake says a lot about his or her personality. So, be sure to shake hands with confidence:

- Extend and shake with your right hand.
- When you put out your hand, extend your fingers and point your thumb up.
- When you make contact with the other person's hand, close your fingers around it and lower your thumb.
- Your grip should be firm but not aggressive.
- Hold onto the other person's hand for about three seconds. Then pull your hand away naturally.
- During the whole handshake, smile at the other person and look him or her in the eye!

2. **When you meet others in the workplace, look them in the eye, smile, and shake hands.** Making eye contact suggests that you are confident and eager. Smiling suggests that you are friendly and pleased to meet someone. And shaking hands is an expected greeting in the workplace when meeting both men and women.

3. *Concentrate* **on learning your job throughout the day.** Put all your effort toward doing things correctly. But don't worry if you don't do everything right on the first day. It takes a while to learn any job. Show that you are trying hard and willing to learn. And don't be shy about asking questions or asking for help. Your efforts will be noticed.

Concentrate

To think hard about something or pay close attention to something.

4. **Be on time.** Arrive at the workplace a few minutes early, so that you're ready to start on time. Go to lunch and take your breaks when you're supposed to. And then, don't take longer than you should or be late getting back. Both supervisors and co-workers notice these things! Also, bad habits are easy to form and hard to break.

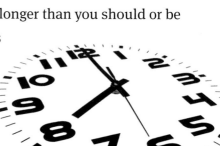

5. **Don't expect or ask for special favors.** Don't expect your supervisor to give you extra time or special attention. Remember that you're one of a group of employees. Also, don't expect your co-workers to do your work or to

cover for you. For instance, never ask a co-worker to lie about your being late or leaving early.

6. **Do work that you're proud of.** When it comes to your work, never settle for "good enough." Try hard to do a little bit better every day. Developing your work skills and abilities can be a real challenge. But over time, you'll discover the rewards that can come from doing well in the workplace.

CHAPTER 2

The Employee Handbook

When you start your job, your supervisor may give you an employee handbook. If you don't receive a handbook, it's a good idea to ask if one is available. It's sometimes called the *employee manual*, and it's sometimes available online.

What's So Important about an Employee Handbook?

Having an employee handbook protects both the employee and the employer. The handbook outlines important company policies. It tells employees what their employer expects of them. It also tells employees what to expect of their employer. And when expectations aren't met, everyone knows what will happen—because it's stated in the handbook. In this way, the employee handbook helps create a fair and consistent working environment. Having a handbook helps avoid conflicts and prevent unnecessary lawsuits.

Basic Information

The employee handbook contains basic information you should know about your job and your workplace. A typical handbook tells about company **policies**. For instance, it explains things such as time sheets and shift times, sick leave, vacations and holidays, and the locations of supplies. It's designed to answer questions new employees might ask, such as these:

Policies

Rules or guidelines.

→ How do I report the extra hours I've worked so I'll get paid overtime?

→ How can I get a parking permit for the company lot?

→ How many days of paid vacation do I get a year?

Employee Evaluations

The employee handbook may also explain how and when employee *evaluations* are done. These evaluations are sometimes called *performance reviews*. At your performance review or evaluation, your supervisor will give you his or her opinion about your work. He or she will probably show you a form that contains ratings or grades about specific things you do in your job.

Evaluation
A review to determine the value of someone or something.

Precautions
Steps taken to provide safety and avoid problems.

Safety Information

The employee handbook may also explain safety *precautions* you should take to protect yourself in the workplace. And it will likely explain what to do if you're injured on the job. For example, it will probably tell you where to get help and how to call for emergency care if you've been exposed to chemicals. The handbook may also tell you where to find first aid supplies or how to help injured co-workers.

Complaints and Concerns

The employee handbook may also contain information on filing a grievance. A *grievance* is a formal statement of complaint or concern. Most workplaces have specific **procedures** for filing a grievance. Following those procedures will help your employer respond to your complaint or concern.

Grievances are sometimes filed in cases of *harassment*. To be *harassed* is to be repeatedly bothered or annoyed by someone else. At work, it may be another employee

Procedures

Methods or systems of doing things.

who keeps asking you to go on a date. Or it might be someone who's touching you or hanging around you all the time. It might even be someone who's interfering with your work so you won't get credit for it.

In any case, you shouldn't feel helpless. If you decide to file a grievance, someone will investigate the problem and offer a solution.

Dealing with Harassment

If you're being harassed on the job, keep track of what happens. You'll need these details to file a grievance. You'll also need them to prove your case against whoever is harassing you. Follow these tips:

- **Carry a notebook.** Write down every harassing act, large or small.

- **Be detailed.** Record as many details as possible, such as specific dates and times. Also write down everything that was said and done.

- **Write down names.** Write down the names of everyone involved. Include the names of people who might have witnessed the harassment.

- **Make copies.** Make copies of all your notes, and keep them in a safe place.

- **Save voice recordings.** Save recordings, such as harassing voicemails.

Read the Handbook!

Read the whole handbook the first or second day of your job. If you don't understand something, ask questions of your supervisor or human resources director. It's a good idea to get everything clear in your mind early in your employment. Knowing this information will help you to stay both satisfied and safe on the job.

Some companies have new employees sign a form saying they received a copy of the handbook. Companies do this so employees can't say later that they didn't know about workplace policies and procedures. Be sure to get a handbook and keep it where you'll be able to use it.

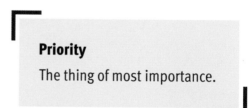

CHAPTER 3

Fitting In with Co-Workers

A big part of your job satisfaction will come from your relationships with your co-workers. Not all those relationships will be the same. You'll really like some of your co-workers and want to be friends with them outside work. But you won't like other people nearly as well. Just being around them might be challenging for you.

When you're at work, your first *priority* is to do your job as well as you can. And that means you should try to get along with everyone.

Priority

The thing of most importance.

Be a Good Co-Worker

When you meet your fellow employees, concentrate on remembering their names. Also try to notice who does what. Pay attention to people's job titles and responsibilities. And as you go about your job, notice how your co-workers do their jobs, too.

Check in with the company's supply clerk to learn how to **restock** your own work supplies. Do this on a regular basis, such as weekly or monthly. Sometimes, it may be tempting to "borrow" supplies from co-workers. But even if you're in a rush, be sure to ask first. Don't just take something—such as a pair of scissors or a wrench—that someone else will need. Your co-worker may be annoyed or **inconvenienced** if you take something without permission.

Finally, stay in your own work area. If you're always "visiting" someone else's workspace, then neither of you is doing your work. If you annoy your co-workers, they may react by avoiding you or complaining about you.

Restock

To replace supplies that have been taken or used up.

Inconvenienced

Bothered or uncomfortable. To *inconvenience* someone is to create a problem or make something difficult for him or her.

Topics to Avoid in the Workplace

A number of topics are considered inappropriate when talking with co-workers. And choosing the wrong topic can affect how you are thought of and treated in the workplace. Here's a list of topics to avoid:

- Family and marriage problems
- Health problems
- Religion
- Politics
- Sex
- Salary or wages
- Career goals
- Complaints about work

Know What NOT to Talk About

Don't talk about your personal life while at work. No one needs to know that your girlfriend is mad at you or that you talked a police officer out of giving you a speeding ticket. Also avoid talking about things that might annoy or offend someone. Keep your personal opinions to yourself.

Be aware of gossip. It exists at every company, and getting involved in it can be tempting. For instance, you may want to agree with a complaint you hear about the company's vacation policy. Or you may be curious about a co-worker's personal life. It's best not to get involved in such conversations. If you do, someone might say that you're taking sides or spreading negative information.

Tips for Avoiding Gossip at Work

- Don't share personal information about yourself or others.
- Stay away from the people and places involved in gossip.
- Change the subject when the conversation turns to gossip.
- Don't pass on the gossip you hear.
- Challenge people who gossip.

[FACT]

Facts about Office Gossip

- The average employee spends 65 hours a year gossiping with co-workers. That comes to almost $500 in lost time for someone doing a minimum-wage job.

- 66% of employees admit to gossiping about company news.

- 28% of employees say that gossip is their main source of information about their employer.

- The most common place for exchanging office gossip is the employee break room (36%). The second most common place is at employees' desks or in their offices (33%).

- Gossip generally takes two forms: news about changes at the company and personal stories about company employees.

Be Positive

When you're at work, stay focused on what you were hired to do. Set daily goals for the things you want to accomplish. Challenge yourself to do a little more each day. But keep in mind what your priorities should be. What does your supervisor want you to do first, second, and so on?

Of course, you should be friendly and helpful to others when you can. Look for opportunities to help out, especially with new co-workers. And remember that good manners count. It's never a mistake to be considerate or to thank someone who's helped you.

Getting along with your co-workers is important. In the long run, your work experience will be as positive as *you* make it.

CHAPTER **4**

Interpreting a Paycheck

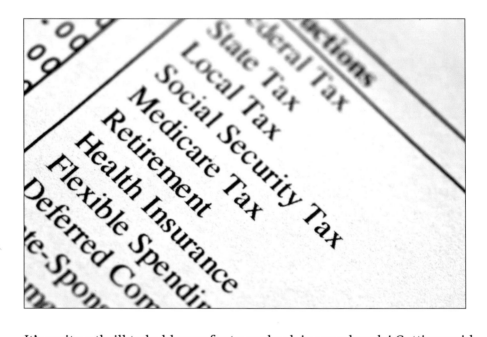

It's quite a thrill to hold your first paycheck in your hands! Getting paid makes all of your hard work seem worthwhile.

Many employers offer *direct deposit* of your **earnings**. That means the employer will put the money directly into your bank account. You don't have to pick up your check or take it to the bank to deposit it. You can take your check to the bank if you want to, however.

The Earnings Statement

However you decide to get paid, you'll receive an earnings **statement**. It's attached to your check and is sometimes called the *check stub*. Your wages or salary is listed on the earnings statement. It's called *gross pay*. In financial terms, the word *gross* means "total" or "overall."

The amount you actually receive is less than your gross pay. *Deductions* are withheld from your earnings. Deductions are amounts of money taken out of your earnings to pay for other things. Deductions are sometimes called *withholdings*.

The amount left after all the deductions have been made is called your *net pay*. In financial terms, the word *net* means "remaining." Net pay is sometimes referred to as *take-home pay*.

Earnings

The money someone gets paid for doing work. The word *earnings* is sometimes used instead of *salary*, *wages*, *pay*, or *income*.

Statement

A financial record that shows additions and subtractions of money for a certain time period.

Deductions

Two deductions from your gross pay are required by the US government:

1. **Federal income tax:** This is the money you pay to support the nation's government. Income tax is a percentage of what you earn.

2. **Social Security or FICA:** This is the money you contribute to a fund that supports senior citizens, people with disabilities, and others in need. When you retire, you'll be able to get money from this fund.

[FACT]

Federal Income Tax

Federal income tax is a percentage of your annual earnings. The rate is different for people that earn different amounts of money. It's also different for people who are single versus married, who have children, and so on. In 2011, a single person with no children paid these federal income tax rates:

Earnings	Rate	Earnings	Rate
$8,500 or less	10%	$83,601–$174,400	28%
$8,501–$34,500	15%	$174,401–$379,150	33%
$34,501–$83,600	25%	$379,151 and over	35%

You'll probably see other deductions on your earnings statement, too:

→ **State income tax** is the money taken from your earnings to support your state government. Not all states require their residents to pay an income tax, but most do.

→ Deductions for **health insurance** and **dental insurance** go into plans that help pay your doctor and dentist bills.

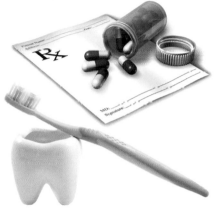

→ The **disability insurance** deduction goes into a plan that pays employees who can't work because of injury or illness. You would get paid if you got seriously hurt or sick.

→ Some people have money withheld for **donations to charities**. For example, many people give money to the United Way. That charity supports local organizations that help people in need.

→ Workers who belong to a *union* have their union dues deducted.

→ Some people have money withheld and put into a **savings account**. Doing so is a sure way to build up your savings.

Union

An organization of workers. The organization is formed to protect workers' common goals and to improve their working conditions.

Sample Earnings Statement

Every company or organization has its own list of deductions. Rick Marshall works for the Applegate Cannery. His earnings statement is shown below.

5015

APPLEGATE CANNERY

Rick Marshall
June 1–15, 2011

Gross Pay $895.00

Deductions:
Federal income tax $98.45
FICA   71.60
Health insurance   107.40
United Way   3.00
Union dues   32.00

Net Pay $582.55

Your earnings statement won't look exactly like Rick's. But you'll find some of the same *categories* of deductions listed.

Why should you know how to read your earnings statement? It's important for two reasons: to understand what all the deductions are for and to make sure the amount is correct.

When you begin a new job, it's a good idea to talk to the payroll clerk or whoever writes employees' checks. Make sure that all your information is correct.

Categories

Groups or types. Items are placed into *categories* based on their similarities.

[FACT]

What Will Social Security Pay You?

You'll pay into the Social Security fund during all the years that you work. You'll be able to receive Social Security payments after you reach the retirement age of 65. How much you receive from Social Security each month will depend on how much money you earn in your lifetime. The Social Security Administration (SSA) uses a formula to calculate this amount. It's based on the 35-year period that you earned the most money. You can keep track of this amount by looking at the yearly statement that's sent out by the SSA. You'll start getting this statement when you turn 25.

Learning the Job

Starting a new job involves learning new skills. But it also involves applying skills you may already have in new ways. For instance, most jobs require having good communication skills. And most jobs require working with other people, including supervisors and co-workers. You'll get off to a good start at your new job if you learn how to apply some key skills.

Learning to Do Things Right

Jackson waited nervously at his desk. Karen, his supervisor, was due to get out of her meeting at any time. And he was afraid that she was going to be upset with him.

Two hours earlier, Karen had asked Jackson to update some employee records on the computer. She was going to have performance reviews with these employees later in the week. But she wanted to have their records updated today. That way, she'd have time to review the information over the next few days.

Karen had told Jackson what to do. But after he'd left her office, he realized that he didn't understand. He had Karen's notes about the updates that were needed. But he wasn't sure where the employee records were stored on the computer. He also wasn't sure who was supposed to check his work and sign off on the updated records. He'd only worked at the company for a month, and he hadn't done this kind of task before. If he could just remember all the things Karen had said!

When Karen got out of her meeting, Jackson planned to ask her to repeat the directions. But this time, he'd write down the key points. He'd also ask some questions to make sure he understood exactly what needed to be done.

As it turned out, Karen wasn't upset with Jackson. She said that she was glad he'd asked for help. Delaying the work for a few hours was much better than having it done incorrectly, she told him.

CHAPTER **1**

Impressing Your Supervisor

Once you've gotten your job, you face your next major challenge: How can you **impress** your supervisor? What can you do to get **recognized**? How can you make sure you won't be fired? What do you have to do to get a promotion or raise?

Impress
To have a strong, positive effect on someone.

Recognized
Known for your positive qualities or good work.

Know about Your Company

Pay attention to news about your company. For instance, maybe your company is doing well and plans to hire more people. Or maybe it's involved in community events. Watch for stories in the local newspaper and on the local TV news. Also look for information on the company's Web site. Being interested in the company will show that you take your job there seriously.

Depending on what job you have, you may never meet your company's leaders. But it's still a good idea to know the names of the president, chairperson of the board, and so on. It's also a good idea to know the names of department heads and other key people. Knowing these people's names will help you recognize them when you read and hear about your company.

Before You Start

Prepare to impress your supervisor even *before* your first day at work. Learn everything you can about the company. Talk to other people who work there. Read about it online. Find answers to questions such as these:

→ How many employees does the company have?

→ Does it have offices, warehouses, or sales groups in other locations?

→ Who uses the company's services or products and why?

→ How long has the company been in business?

In other words, make the effort to be as well informed as possible. Your supervisor is sure to notice that you've taken the time and energy to learn about the company. That shows you're taking your job seriously. And knowing this information about the company will help you in your day-to-day tasks.

On the Job

You can do many things to prove that you're **genuinely** trying to be a good worker:

1. **Pay attention.** Learn how the best workers do their jobs. Take notes at meetings. Think. Ask questions about company goals, products, and services. Show that you want to know as much as possible about how *your* work fits into the company's plans.

> **Genuinely**
> Honestly or seriously.

2. **Be prepared for meetings.** Make sure you get to meetings on time. Bring along some paper and a pen, so you can take notes. Also, bring along any material that may help with the discussion.

Guidelines for Good Meetings

1. Take meetings seriously. Show up on time, pay attention, and stay for the entire meeting.
2. Be prepared. Bring along the *agenda*, or plan, for the meeting. Also bring a pen and notebook.
3. Stay on topic. Don't have personal conversations. And don't talk about work topics that not everyone needs to know about.
4. Be honest. Take the opportunity to state your opinion or to share what you know.
5. Follow through. After the meeting, do what you're supposed to do.

3. **Volunteer.** Suppose your supervisor asks for volunteers to help work on a special project. By all means, volunteer. Doing so is a great way to show your enthusiasm and gain more experience.

4. **Do good work.** Do your very best to turn out a good product or service. Be agreeable when asked to do something extra. And always speak up if you're asked for your opinion. Make suggestions and share ideas you have for improvements. No one will know your *capabilities* if you never share what you think and know.

5. **Be patient.** Finally, realize that it usually takes time to get recognized for your good work. But be confident that it *will* happen.

> **Capabilities**
> Abilities or talents.

Communicate Confidence!

A lot of what we communicate to others comes from our actions, not our words. Be sure to communicate confidence in the way you carry yourself:

- **Make eye contact.** Looking people in the eye shows that you're comfortable talking to them. It also shows that you're interested and paying attention. And it shows that you're open and honest. Not looking people in the eye shows all the opposites: that you're uneasy, not interested, not paying attention, and maybe even dishonest.

- **Smile.** Smiling in a natural way shows warmth and friendliness. Smiling at other people puts them at ease. Not smiling indicates worry, fear, or unhappiness. And smiling in an unnatural way indicates nervousness or dishonesty.

- **Nod your head.** When listening to other people talk, nod your head slightly. It shows that you're focused and interested in what's being said. It also shows that you understand and support what's being said. Frowning suggests that you don't understand or agree.

- **Stand and sit up straight.** Standing or sitting up straight shows that you are secure in your surroundings. It also shows that you're paying attention and ready to participate. Slouching indicates that you're distracted and unsure of yourself.

- **Use your hands when you speak.** Making natural gestures while you speak shows energy and confidence. Not knowing what to do with your hands makes you seem uncomfortable or shy. And making wild or jerky gestures makes you look nervous.

CHAPTER 2

Following Verbal Directions and Asking for Clarification

Tomás is a new employee in a warehouse. So far, he's spent most of his time stacking crates with a forklift. But this morning, Tomás's supervisor, Mark, gave him a specific job to do.

Mark told Tomás, "You need to make room for a new shipment. Move the TVs from the platform next to Building A. Take them to Building C, and stack them up on the top level."

"We've got TVs in both Buildings B and C," Tomás told Mark. "You want me to move all of them to C?"

"No," Mark said. "Just the ones here in A."

"Then I'll need to enter it on the inventory for Building C, right?" Tomás asked.

"Right," said Mark.

"You want me to move them right away?" Tomás asked.

"Yep, just as soon as you can," Mark replied.

Understanding Verbal Directions

Mark gave Tomás **verbal** directions. When someone gives you directions that way, it's important to pay close attention. Spoken directions can easily be misunderstood.

How can you make sure you understand what you're being told? Listen for *what* and *how* and *when*. In the example about Tomás, these are the key pieces of information:

> **Verbal**
>
> Spoken or said out loud.

→ **What** exactly does his supervisor want him to do?

→ **How** should he do it?

→ **When** does his supervisor expect it to be done?

Asking for Clarification

If you don't understand verbal directions, ask questions right away. Asking for **clarification** shows that you want to do the job correctly. And most supervisors are willing to repeat the directions or explain them more clearly. Providing clarification will avoid having the work done incorrectly.

Tomás was confused about which TVs to move—so he asked Mark for clarification. Tomás double-checked to make sure he wasn't supposed to move the TVs in Building B. And he asked if he should start that task immediately.

Use Learning Tools

When verbal directions are too brief or too **complicated**, it's best to write them down. That way, you'll have something written to refer to. It might also help you to make a drawing to help you remember information. Think of other tools you can use to help you understand verbal directions.

Clarification
Information provided to make something clear or easier to understand.

Complicated
Confusing or difficult.

Tomás made a simple map to help him remember Mark's directions. The map showed Buildings A, B, and C. Tomás added lines to show the trips he'd make in moving the TVs. Having a map built Tomás's *confidence*. He knew he wouldn't get mixed up.

After reviewing the map for a few minutes, Tomás started moving the TVs. He finished the job so quickly that Mark had him help co-workers with some of their work.

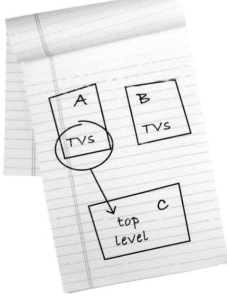

Confidence

The sense of believing in one's own abilities.

What's Your Learning Style?

The way that you learn best is your *learning style*. There are three general styles:

1. **Visual** learners like to see and look. They learn well by reading and taking notes. They usually prefer a quiet workplace.

2. **Auditory** learners like to hear and listen. They learn well by having things explained to them. They often hum or talk to themselves and don't mind background noise.

3. **Kinesthetic** learners like to touch and do. They learn well by putting things together or handling materials. They like to move around and may have trouble sitting still.

Memorization Tricks

Use memorization tricks to help you remember important information. These tricks are called *mnemonics* (pronounced "neh-MAHN-iks"). Here are some examples you may know:

- The names of the Great Lakes (Superior, Michigan, Huron, Erie, Ontario): "Super Man Helps Every One."

- The names and order of the planets (Mercury, Venus, Earth, Mars, Jupiter, Saturn, Uranus, Neptune): My Very Educated Mother Just Served Us Noodles.

- The names of musical notes on the lines (E, G, B, D, F): "Every Good Boy Deserves Fun."

- The order of the operations in math (parentheses, exponents, multiplication, division, addition, subtraction): "Please Excuse My Dear Aunt Sally."

CHAPTER 3

Reading Instructions: Using a Job Aid

Cooks read the orders that servers hand them. Delivery drivers read maps. Carpenters read blueprints. Railroad workers read lists of cars that make up a train.

Having good reading skills is important in almost every job. You may need to master several kinds of reading skills for your job.

Make Use of Instructions

Briona works as an administrative assistant. On her first day, she was asked to photocopy a 48-page report for an important meeting. The copy machine was more complicated than any copier Briona had ever seen. She had no idea how to work it! But she kept calm. She pressed a button that lit up the instructions on the copier's screen. After reading them carefully, Briona followed the steps, one after another. By taking things one step at a time—and not *panicking*—Briona was able to do the job. She turned out good copies in time for the meeting.

On the roof of Briona's office building, Jason, a sheet metal worker, was *installing* an air conditioner. He'd helped his boss install this model once before. But today he was on his own—and he was stuck! Two important parts simply wouldn't fit together. Jason knew better than to

Panicking
Having a strong feeling of fear or worry.

Install
To put in place or set up for use.

force them. Feeling ***desperate***, he opened the instruction manual. By reading the instructions carefully, he discovered the problem. He needed a connector that was still in the packing crate! Once he located the missing part, Jason completed the job and felt satisfied. Next time, he'd know *exactly* how to do the whole installation.

Briona's boyfriend, Ty, got a job taking phone orders at a mail order company. All day long, he sat at a computer, wearing a headset and talking on the phone. After a few weeks, Ty's neck began to hurt. His supervisor gave him written guidelines about ergonomics. *Ergonomics* is the study of the safest, most comfortable ways for people to use equipment at work. By reading the guidelines, Ty realized that his neck was hurting because his computer monitor was too

Desperate
Having lost hope or being in great need.

high. He lowered the screen, and after just a few days, the **_discomfort_** in his neck had disappeared.

No matter what your job is, you'll need to solve a problem from time to time. Often, you'll be able to solve the problem easily if you know how to read and follow written instructions. Think of directions as friends who guide you until you're sure of how to do something on your own!

If you can't figure out how to solve a problem on your own, ask for help. Maybe one of your co-workers will know what to do. If not, go to your supervisor. Don't look at needing help as a sign of weakness or lack of competence. In fact, it takes self-confidence to ask for and accept help.

Discomfort

A feeling of uneasiness or stress. _Discomfort_ can be physical or mental.

Become a Better Reader

According to the US Department of Education, 32 million adults don't have basic reading skills. That's about 1 in 7 American adults. These individuals can't read an article in the newspaper or the directions on a bottle of medicine. They also struggle at work. Many stay in low-level jobs or lose jobs because they can't read.

A lot of Web sites provide free help to adults who want to become better readers. These five sites offer lesson plans, activities, handbooks, and practice tests online:

1. Scholastic: www.scholastic.com

2. PBS Teachers: www.pbs.org

3. Literacy Connections: www.literacyconnections.com

4. Thirteen Ed: www.thirteen.org

5. McGraw Hill: www.mcgrawhill.com

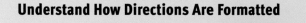

Understand How Directions Are Formatted

Understanding how directions are set up on the printed page will help you make sense of them. Look for these common features:

- **Titles and headings:** The title usually appears across the top of the page. Headings break up the page into main sections.

- **Lists:** Lists are used to split information into separate points or sentences. A numbered list usually means the information presents the steps or parts of something.

- **Bold type and capital letters:** Bold type and capital letters show that something is important.

- **Type size:** In general, big type is more important than small type. However, small type often includes important details.

- **Photos and diagrams:** Photos and diagrams show what's being described by the text.

CHAPTER 4

Teamwork and Cooperation

Anyone who's ever played a sport knows about teamwork. It's the group effort that results in winning the game. All the team members pull together to achieve the team's common goal.

Teamwork is part of most jobs, too. Whether you work in an office or a factory, you'll likely be part of a team. And your team's success will require ***cooperation***.

> **Cooperation**
> Working well together to achieve a common goal.

Types of Team Members

Suppose your supervisor asks you to participate in a group planning session. What will you do?

Workers respond to requests like this in a variety of ways. Some workers contribute a lot. Some sit and listen but say or do very little. And still others contribute nothing, hoping their co-workers will do all the work.

Of course, the best type of *participation* is the first: to contribute a lot. So, how do you make a strong *contribution* as a team member, especially if you are a new employee?

Participate
To take part in.

Contribution
The work someone does or the effort he or she makes toward achieving a common goal with others.

Making a Strong Contribution

1. **Pay attention.** You need to thoroughly understand the project everyone is discussing. What does your supervisor expect the team to accomplish? Perhaps your team is planning a new product, such as a different type of baked goods at a small bakery. Or maybe you're improving a service, such as helping bank customers with their most frequent needs. Or perhaps your group is designing a long-term plan, such as adding more recreational classes at a community center. Whatever the team is doing, make sure you are clear about the project's goals

2. **Be a good teammate.** At group meetings, express your willingness to coop-erate. Contribute your ideas, but don't take over the discussion. Listen to what others say, and be open to their suggestions. Don't insist on doing things your own way. *Compromise* when it seems appropriate. You might even suggest combining your idea with someone else's to make a good plan.

Compromise
A settlement that's reached after each side agrees to give up some of what it wants.

3. **Know the deadlines.** As your team's plan goes into action, stay aware of any deadlines you have to meet. Write them down on a calendar or planner, or enter them on the calendar on your computer or phone. Make sure everyone knows these key dates. Also understand that not all team members will likely work at the same pace. Keep this in mind when planning work assignments. Try to give individuals tasks that they will do well. But if needed, be ready to help co-workers complete their tasks.

Remember that your team's goal is to successfully complete the project within the required time period. Recognize that each person's contribution should be valued for its role in the team's success. Show respect for others' efforts. And compliment those who contribute extra time and energy.

How Teams Come Together

No team or group works well together right from the start! All go through four stages on their way to working successfully:

1. **Forming** involves meeting everyone and setting up procedures.

2. **Storming** involves conflict among team members, as roles and goals are determined.

3. **Norming** is the stage when team members have figured out how to work together.

4. **Performing** occurs when the team works successfully in all areas.

All teams go through these stages but not necessarily at the same pace. Teams that are disorganized and lack leadership may stay in the "forming" stage for a while. Teams whose members disagree and compete with one another may get stuck in the "storming" stage. Teams that have trouble coming together may spend little time in the "performing" stage before they're done with their assignment.

Guidelines for Getting Along

- If possible, don't have an official team leader. Share leadership or take turns.

- Encourage everyone to express opinions, and value what people say.

- Identify the strengths and skills of individual team members. Then assign responsibilities based on them.

- Meet on a regular basis and in the same place, if possible.

- Agree on how you will make decisions.

- Have clear expectations for what each individual will contribute.

- At difficult times, remind team members of their common goals and achievements.

Succeeding on the Job

Most workers are evaluated by their employers once a year. But why wait? You can evaluate yourself and figure out what you need to do to improve your job performance. By setting your own goals and working hard to achieve them, you can succeed on the job. And in doing that, you can put yourself in the position to get what every employee wants: a raise!

Planning to Get Ahead

Kim was working full time and taking a class three mornings a week. That didn't leave him much free time! But he believed all his hard work would pay off.

His performance review was in two months, and he hoped it would result in a promotion. The position of assistant store manager was opening up. If Kim got the job, it would mean a raise. It would also mean he'd get some benefits, including health insurance.

Kim had worked at Mario's Men's Store for almost a year. He'd started as a part-time sales associate, working 25 hours a week. But after only a few months, the store manager,

Kelly, asked if he'd be available full time. She said she liked the fact that he found things to do in the store when sales were slow. Several of his co-workers just stood around and talked when they weren't busy with customers.

After Kim started working full time, Kelly gave him more responsibilities. She also listened to his suggestions for how to display items in the store. And together, they worked out a checklist of things for employees to do during slow periods.

Kim knew that the position of assistant manager involved recording each day's sales. So he signed up for a class at the community college to learn basic accounting skills. Kelly agreed to shift his hours at the store so he'd be free to take the class. She believed in him and wanted to support his going to school. She wished all her employees showed the promise that Kim did!

CHAPTER **1**

Measurements of Progress

For six months, Hannah had been working as a hairstylist at a small salon. And she could tell she was making progress.

For instance, Hannah had learned to be more ***efficient***. Now, by carefully ***scheduling*** her appointments, she was using her time well. She arranged her appointments in blocks of time. That way, she didn't spend hours each day waiting for her next appointment. And when Hannah did have time between appointments, she took care of other tasks. She ordered styling products, organized her workstation, and so on. She didn't waste a minute!

Efficient
Getting things done without wasting time or money.

Scheduling
Planning or arranging for things to happen at certain times.

Clients
The people who use the services or products of a business. *Clients* are sometimes called *customers*.

Having a set schedule also helped Hannah pick up more regular **clients**. People liked the fact that she was available at certain times of day. Many of them set up appointments weeks in advance. Many of them also told their friends about Hannah, and the friends became clients, too.

Having more clients meant that Hannah's income was steadily increasing. She was proud to be able to save part of her salary. She thought about buying a townhouse in a few years.

But Hannah's greatest satisfaction came from making her clients happy. She knew they were pleased with the way she did their hair. Some customers had told her they'd never felt better about the way they looked!

Well Done

Evaluating Yourself

It's great to experience a sense of success on the job. Knowing that you're good at what you do builds confidence. But what if your job doesn't involve a growing list of clients? What if you're not seeing a steady increase in your paycheck? How do you know if you're making progress?

It's not hard. You can evaluate how well you're doing by asking yourself these questions:

→ **Am I on my way to becoming an independent worker?** Being *independent* means being able to do your work without constantly asking someone else for help. Once you become confident of what you're doing, you won't need someone to guide you every step of the way.

→ **Do I catch and correct my own mistakes?** No one's perfect. That's why it's important to catch your own mistakes and know how to correct them. If someone else is finding your mistakes, then you need to put more effort into your work. Make sure it meets the standards or expectations of your company, service, or organization. Don't ever take the attitude that "someone else can fix it."

→ **Do I finish on time?** If you do good work within the time allowed for the job, then you're meeting the company's expectations. If you finish early and still do good work, then you're showing even greater *competence*.

→ **Do I have a growing sense of accomplishment?** If you feel that you're doing something worthwhile and take pride in your work, it will show. And even more importantly, your self-esteem will blossom. Having greater self-confidence will help you wherever you work and whatever job you do.

Competence
Skill or ability.

Having Healthy Self-Esteem

Your *self-esteem* is your overall opinion of yourself. It's based on how you feel about your abilities and successes, along with your limitations and failures.

People with healthy self-esteem value themselves. They believe other people should respect them and treat them well. And they generally expect good things to happen.

People with low self-esteem tend to feel that they're not good enough. They worry about pleasing others, and they don't expect to be treated well in return. In fact, these people often expect bad things to happen.

Is it possible to have too high an opinion of yourself? Yes, and it's not healthy. Some people have an unrealistic idea of their skills and accomplishments. And at some point, they will probably be very disappointed by a failure.

Learn from Your Mistakes

Ask these three questions to help learn from the mistakes you make on the job:

1. **Why did I make the mistake?** New employees usually make mistakes because they don't know how to do something. Employees who've been on the job for a while usually make mistakes because they're not paying attention.

2. **How can I correct the mistake?** If you know how to correct your mistake, then do it. If you don't know or need help, then ask for assistance.

3. **What else can I learn?** Mistakes provide opportunities to learn more about your job. They also provide opportunities to talk with your supervisor and co-workers.

CHAPTER **2**

Benchmarks:
Speed and Accuracy

Of course, it's important to do your work correctly. But it's also important to get your work done on time.

Achieving one goal without the other won't help you succeed. If you make mistakes by going too fast, your *output* won't be satisfactory. Going too slowly may stop you from making errors, but your work will be late. Your goal should be to do errorless work that's finished on time.

To judge how well you're doing at work, figure out how your skills match up against your co-workers' skills. Are you more skilled than they are? Or are you less skilled? If you need to improve your skills, ask your supervisor for tips.

Developing Better Keyboarding Skills

Tanya was a clerk in a used bookstore. She helped to keep track of the books the store bought. Working on the computer, she entered each book's title, author, publisher, and date of publication. She also entered the purchase date and the price. Every entry had to be correct. The store used the list to sell books online.

Tanya keyed in the information very *accurately*. But she worked much more slowly than the other two clerks. Her supervisor showed Tanya some exercises to practice on the keyboard. After practicing for a week or so, Tanya was able to work faster. And she was still able to make accurate entries.

"Remember," her supervisor told her, "practice makes perfect."

Benchmarks	**Accuracy**	**Output**
Standards of quality or acceptance.	Correctness and exactness.	What is made or produced.

Learning Basic Office Skills

Many community colleges offer programs for training in basic office skills. Someone who completes the program will earn a Basic Office Skills Certificate (BOSC). This training is intended for people who want entry-level jobs in offices. Those jobs include receptionist, administrative assistant, and general office clerk. BOSC programs include courses in technology and communication skills.

Developing Better Carpentry Skills

Mike went to work as a carpenter's trainee—someone who's learning how to do a job. The contractor who hired him was building a house.

Mike was assigned to work under the supervision of Kent, a more experienced carpenter. The two of them were supposed to cut long boards into beams to hold up the roof. The beams were needed right away, the contractor said.

Mike quickly marked a board to cut. But in his hurry, he didn't place his tape measure on the board correctly. Kent stopped him.

"That will be too short," Kent said. "Measure it again. We need it now, but you'll waste material if you don't take the time to do it right."

Then Kent added, "Have you ever heard the old saying 'Measure twice, cut once'? If you measure once and cut the wrong length, you don't get a second chance."

Learning Basic Carpentry Skills

You can learn basic carpentry skills in several ways:

1. **Watch educational videos.** They are available online or for rent at many building centers. Then practice what you've learned.

2. **Read books and watch TV programs about carpentry and remodeling.** Then again, follow up with practice.

3. **Offer to help with a building project at the home of a friend or family member.** Pay attention to what the most skilled workers are doing.

4. **Volunteer for a program such as Habitat for Humanity.** Learn basic carpentry skills while you help build homes for people in need.

Meeting Your Own Benchmarks

In addition to speed and accuracy, your job will have its own bench-marks. Whatever they are, you'll be rewarded if you *strive* to meet those standards.

But what if you don't meet those standards? What should you do? First of all, get some help. Ask your supervisor to work with you to develop your skills. Also ask him or her to suggest a course or training program you can take. Then, put in the time and effort needed to improve.

Second, don't give up. Learn from your mistakes, and then move on. Continue to strive to do your best. You'll get there!

Strive

To try very hard.

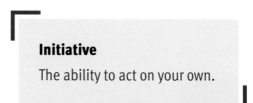

Well Done

CHAPTER **3**

Taking Initiative

Imagine that you're a supervisor at French's Office Supply Store. You see that one of your employees, Sameer, does his job well and shows up on time. He's also pleasant to work with and doesn't fool around on the job. Other people seem to like him, too.

There's one thing that *really* impresses you, though: Sameer takes **initiative** at work. That means he gets things going without being told what to do.

Initiative

The ability to act on your own.

Top-10 Work Values That Employers Look For

1. Strong work ethic
2. Dependability and responsibility
3. Positive attitude
4. Flexibility
5. Honesty and trustworthiness
6. Ability to take initiative
7. Desire to learn
8. Self-confidence
9. Professionalism
10. Loyalty

Solving Problems

Sameer always tries to solve problems that come up. He thinks about the store's goals when he's working. That helps him come up with good ideas. His ideas aren't complicated or difficult, but they work. Plus, they show that he's always thinking.

Here's an example: As Sameer's supervisor, you were disappointed in the sales of a hot new item. It was a laptop bag that had been on the shelf for a week. You thought it should have attracted more attention and sold better.

Sameer had an idea about how to sell more bags. He suggested moving them from the computer supply area to a display just right of the   front door. Sameer had noticed that most customers turned to their right when they entered the store. He thought

that moving the bags there would draw more attention to them.

Sameer was right! At the end of the first day, French's had sold more laptop bags than they'd sold the whole week before.

Keeping Your Job in a Bad Economy

1. Be the person others in the company go to for help and information.

2. Make sure your work is measurable. Also make sure it's noticed by your supervisor and company leaders.

3. Ask for more responsibilities and more challenging projects.

4. Develop a friendly relationship with your supervisor.

5. Don't whine, complain, or cause trouble.

6. Work long hours. Again, make sure your supervisor and others notice.

7. Develop your work skills and your social skills.

8. Cooperate with co-workers to achieve goals and be successful.

Being Efficient

Sameer also took initiative in other ways. He created many *alternative* procedures for getting jobs done. And in most cases, he found a more efficient way to accomplish the same task.

Alternative
Different or optional.

For instance, French's "sale" signs were being thrown in a box of jumbled materials in the storeroom. When someone needed a sign, it took a long time to find one. Sometimes, when a salesperson couldn't find a sign, he or she made a **_duplicate_**. That wasted both time and money.

Sameer set up a big file and put the signs in it. That allowed workers to find signs quickly. It also gave them the chance to spot worn-out signs and replace them, when needed.

Duplicate
Matching or repeated.

Lending a Hand

Another way that Sameer showed initiative was to help out with special projects. For example, someone was needed to help organize the retirement party for the store's co-owner. Sameer volunteered. He

suggested several ways to prepare for the party and help make it run smoothly. He also got some of his co-workers involved. Knowing that he had organized things made them willing to help.

As Sameer's supervisor, you know that if you need someone to take the lead, you can rely on Sameer. And when you think of giving your employees a raise, Sameer will be at the top of the list.

[FACT]

Why People Stay in Their Jobs

A survey of 910 employees asked about their main reasons for staying in their jobs. Here are their answers:

- Interesting job responsibilities (41%)
- Long-term possibilities for growth and success (33%)
- Loyalty to company (15%)
- Salary/Wages and benefits (7%)
- Loyalty to supervisor (4%)

CHAPTER **4**

Qualifying for a Raise

Suppose you've been at your job for three years. Your boss seems to like you OK, but you've never had a raise. You wonder why! Your friend Brady got a raise from his company after only one year.

How can you show your employer that you deserve more money? Remember that most companies don't give raises ***automatically***. They give them to reward highly valued workers.

Automatically
Without thought or by earlier arrangement.

What Does Your Employer Think?

Ask yourself the questions below. They **highlight** the most important qualities your employer will consider when evaluating or judging you for a raise:

→ Is my work output equal to that of my co-workers?

→ Has my attendance been good?

→ Are clients satisfied with my work or service?

→ Have I contributed ideas or provided other information that's benefited the company?

Highlight
To draw attention to or emphasize.

→ Have I volunteered for special projects or done anything extra that had a positive effect on the company?

→ Do I have a good attitude and get along with my co-workers?

Getting a raise often involves having a complete review of your work performance and attitude. In some companies, evaluating employees for raises is done according to strict, particular guidelines. In other companies, the boss may simply decide it's time to reward a *dedicated* and hard-working employee.

Dedicated

Committed to or strongly in support of.

Making Your Case

So, what should you do when you honestly think you should receive a raise? It's OK to discuss it with your supervisor. He or she may tell you about a company policy regarding raises that applies to you. Or, he or she may give you a raise without much discussion.

In some cases, you may need to negotiate. To *negotiate* means to work out a deal. You and your supervisor may be able to reach a compromise that satisfies both of you.

If you decide to talk to your supervisor, make sure you are well prepared. Be ready with plenty of good reasons to prove that you're worth more money!

Tips for Negotiating a Pay Raise

- Don't be afraid! Almost everything in business is negotiable.
- Ask for more than you'd like to receive. But don't be greedy.
- Be prepared. Know what people in similar positions earn.
- Think of the reasons your supervisor might not want to give you a raise. Then come up with ways to change his or her mind.
- Think of your options. If you can't get a raise, maybe you can get better benefits.
- Don't be needy, demanding, or angry. Always be professional and polite.
- Sell yourself! Bring in information about your work that proves you're valuable.

[FACT]

What's an Average Raise?

- In 2011, the average raise was 3%. This was up from 2.5% in 2010 but down from 4% in 2007.

- Also in 2011, the cost of living increased approximately 3.5%. This means the average raise didn't cover how much more it cost to live.

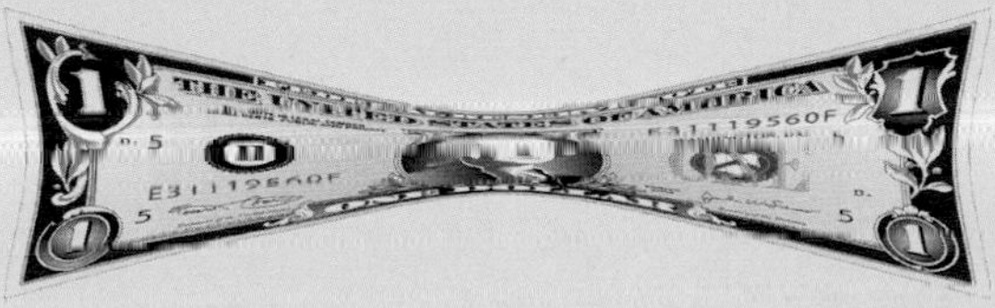

Jobs Likely to Get Good Raises

Administrative Jobs

- Medical records clerk
- Executive assistant
- Customer service representative

Information Technology Jobs

- Network administrator
- Information security manager
- Systems engineer

Finance and Accounting

- Tax accountant
- Compliance director
- Credit manager/supervisor

Workplace Problems and Solutions

People spend a lot of time at work, and not all of that time is pleasant! Sometimes, employees make mistakes and get criticized. Other times, co-workers have annoying habits or bring their personal problems to work with them. You'll be able to stay focused on your work if you know how to deal with common problems in the workplace.

Paying for Other People's Problems

"I need to get out of here!"
Maddie thought to herself.
She'd just come out of a
meeting of the customer service
department, where she worked.
Almost everything they'd talked
about had to do with problems
in the department.

Earlier in the year, the
company had laid off several
employees in customer service.
Because of the layoffs, all the
other employees had to take on
more work. But because of her co-workers' bad habits, Maddie felt that
she'd taken on more work than anyone.

For instance, this morning, Tony was late
again—the third day in a row. His being late
meant that Maddie had to take his phone
calls plus her own. And to make things
worse, Tony had asked her to lie
about what time he'd come in.

Carla was another difficult
co-worker. She was in the middle
of a messy divorce, and she talked
about it all day long. Everyone in the
department knew about Carla's personal

life. Some days, she was on the phone with her lawyer for 30 or 40 minutes at a time. Other days, she was so upset that she went home early. More and more, Maddie was being asked to take on Carla's work.

But the worst of all Maddie's co-workers was Paul. He was constantly making jokes about women. He also made comments about the clothes the women in the office wore. Maddie was offended by his behavior. Sometimes, she did work he was supposed to do, just so she wouldn't have to deal with him.

CHAPTER **1**

Reliability: Tardiness and Absenteeism

A famous comedian once said, "Eighty percent of success in life is showing up." That remark was meant to be funny, of course. But there's some truth to it.

Showing up and being on time are both important in the workplace. Employers expect **reliability** in their employees. Supervisors must be able to count on employees coming to work when they're supposed to. But unfortunately, two common problems in many workplaces are *tardiness* and *absenteeism*.

Tardiness

When an employee is often late, it's usually for one of the following reasons:

1. **Bad sleep habits:** An employee who oversleeps needs to get used to a regular bedtime. For example, suppose Joe has to be at work at 8:00 a.m. and has trouble getting up in the morning. He should get in the habit of going to bed at 10:00 p.m. and getting up at 6:00 a.m. In time, he will get into an eight-hour sleeping pattern that provides enough rest. Then, it will be much easier for him to get up in the morning.

Reliability	Tardiness	Absenteeism
The quality or habit of being dependable and trustworthy.	The quality or habit of being late.	The quality or habit of being gone.

How Much Sleep Do You Need?

Doctors say there is no "magic number" for how much sleep adults need. Instead, the hours of sleep each person requires is based on two things:

1. **Sleep need:** This is how much sleep your body needs on a regular basis for you to perform well. For most adults, it's seven or eight hours a night.

2. **Sleep debt:** This is the total hours of sleep you've lost to being sick, or staying up late.

If you have a large sleep debt, you should try to "pay it down." In other words, you should try to take naps and meet your sleep need for many nights in a row. If you keep a high sleep debt, you will likely feel sleepy and be less sharp than you'd like during the day.

2. **Unreliable transportation:** An employee whose car sometimes doesn't start needs to find alternative transportation. An ***unpredictable*** car might have to be replaced with a dependable bus schedule. How about an employee who rides with a co-worker that's often late? That co-worker should be replaced with one who's ***punctual***.

3. **Poor planning:** Some people don't allow enough time to get ready for work. How long does it take to have a relaxed meal, to shower and get dressed, and to travel to work without being rushed? By noticing exactly how many minutes each activity takes, it's possible

Unpredictable

Acting in a way that is not expected.

Punctual

On time or at the agreed upon time.

to set up a schedule. Caitlin, for example, knows that it takes her 1 hour and 15 minutes to get ready for work. So she starts getting ready 1 hour and 15 minutes before she needs to leave the house.

Absenteeism

When an employee often misses work, it's usually for one of two reasons:

1. **Bad attitude about work:** Employees sometimes think that other parts of their lives are more important than work. And some frequently miss work because they don't like their jobs. If possible, these individuals should find other employment. Otherwise, they need to change their attitude so they can be reliable workers. If all employees went to work only when they "felt like it," companies would certainly fail.

2. **Poor health:** An employee who misses work a lot because of poor health needs to discuss the situation with his or her supervisor. Perhaps they can work together on a plan that will meet the requirements of the job. Maybe the employee's hours can be shortened or some of the work can be done at home. Or the supervisor might suggest that the employee take a temporary leave of absence until his or her health improves.

Talk It Out

No matter what the situation, communication is key. Talk to your supervisor before he or she thinks your absenteeism is a problem. Don't wait for your supervisor to talk to you. By then, your absenteeism will already be a problem. And because of that, there may be fewer options for you and your supervisor to talk about.

CHAPTER 2

Handling Criticism

Connor McCormick is the manager of the shoe department at Swift's Department Store. One day, Mr. Taylor, the store manager, called Connor to his office. He told Connor

> **Criticism**
> A statement of disapproval or negative judgment.

there had been some complaints about his department.

Two customers weren't satisfied with the way they were treated. Both felt they had been ignored, and they were angry about it. One customer even said that she'd spoken to Connor, but he hadn't seemed to care about improving the situation.

Think About What's Said

Mr. Taylor had never criticized Connor before. Connor was shocked and **embarrassed**! Even so, he remained calm and listened. He asked himself these questions:

→ **Is the criticism *valid*?** In other words, is there a **legitimate** reason the customers should be upset?

→ **Is the criticism meant to be *constructive*?** Is Mr. Taylor telling Connor about the problem to help solve it?

Embarrassed
Ashamed or uncomfortable.

Valid
True or correct.

Legitimate
According to reason or standards.

Constructive
Positive or helpful.

Come Up with a Solution

Connor told Mr. Taylor that he would correct the situation so it didn't happen again. He also thanked Mr. Taylor for bringing the problem to his attention.

That day, Connor started working with his salespeople. They discussed several different ways to make sure customers felt satisfied.

After Connor came up with several solutions, he reported back to Mr. Taylor. He explained the new procedures he planned to put in place. He also asked for Mr. Taylor's ideas about the new procedures. Then he thanked Mr. Taylor again for giving him the chance to solve the problem.

Do's and Don'ts for Handling Criticism

Connor handled the situation well. He remained calm until he had enough time to think about the best thing to do.

There are several things Connor could have done to make the situation worse:

→ He could have gotten angry.

→ He could have defended poor work.

→ He could have blamed his salespeople.

→ He could have criticized Mr. Taylor and pointed out his faults.

→ He could have changed the subject and tried to ignore the problem.

None of these responses would have been ***productive***. And perhaps worse, all of these responses would have made Mr. Taylor think poorly of Connor.

What's the most important thing to remember when you're dealing with criticism? *Try to turn it into a positive learning experience.* If you can control whatever anger, hurt, or embarrassment you might feel, you can take time to think. And more times than not, you can turn something bad into something good.

Productive

Helpful or useful.

101

Tips for Handling Criticism at Work

1. **Listen carefully.** Many people shut down when they hear criticism. Instead, listen carefully and take notes.

2. **Don't get emotional.** Again, pay attention. Focus on the facts, not how they make you feel.

3. **Wait to respond.** Don't interrupt. Wait until your supervisor has finished. Then calmly ask what questions you have and explain what you think went wrong. Be brief. Say that you will fix the problem.

4. **Don't hold a grudge.** Don't be mad at your supervisor, and don't pout or complain. Thank your supervisor for pointing out the problem.

5. **Decide how to correct the problem.** Think about what your supervisor said and what you know about the problem. Decide how best to correct it so it won't happen again.

What If You've Been Unfairly Criticized?

No matter how confident you are, you'll probably feel *defensive* after being criticized by your supervisor. You'll get over that feeling if you accept the criticism as valid and constructive. Be sure to take the time to think about these points.

But what if you don't accept it? What if you think you've been criticized unfairly?

Follow these steps:

Defensive

Wanting to defend or protect yourself.

1. When you're listening to the criticism, stay calm. Pay close attention. Take notes, if possible. Above all, don't interrupt!

2. After your supervisor has finished talking, say that you'd like some time to think about his or her comments. Ask if you can meet again in a few days to talk about the problem and how to solve it.

3. Afterward, go somewhere you can be alone. If you took notes, review them. If you didn't take notes, write down the main points of the criticism. Do this now, while you remember what was said.

4. Plan for the follow-up meeting. Write down questions you have about what your supervisor said. Also write down information he or she might not know or did not think about.

5. At the meeting, thank your supervisor for agreeing to talk about the problem. Then present your view. Speak calmly and don't get angry.

6. At the end of the meeting, accept your supervisor's decision—no matter what. Say that you would like to solve the problem. And then follow through by doing what is expected.

CHAPTER **3**

Bringing Personal Problems into the Workplace

One of the benefits of having co-workers is getting to know people and forming friendships. But those friendships should never interfere with doing your work.

Suppose your friend shows up at work very upset. What should you do if she wants your help in solving a personal problem? *Offer to discuss it on your lunch break or after work.*

You'll notice there are generally two kinds of employees in the workplace. Those who always bring their personal problems to work, and those who don't. Make up your mind to be one who *doesn't*.

For example, some co-workers chatter endlessly about their hobbies, their children, or their dates. Some complain about how broke they are or how much it's going to cost to fix the car. Other co-workers continually discuss their health problems. And still others may say they've been up all night and ask you to do some of their work.

Obviously, all of these behaviors prevent people from being reliable workers. Someone whose mind is busy with personal problems can't successfully do his or her job.

Overall, it's important to realize that personal problems don't belong at work. Leave your personal issues at home. Your co-workers shouldn't have to be **distracted** by your life outside the workplace.

Imagine an **invisible** dividing line between your work life and your personal life. That should help to keep the various parts of your life in a **reasonable** and **workable** balance.

Distracted
Unable to think or pay attention.

Invisible
Cannot be seen.

Reasonable
Makes good sense.

Workable
Can be done. Practical and effective.

Tips for Conversations about Personal Problems

- Be positive and supportive. Don't take part in the complaining or criticizing.

- Be logical and objective. Suggest alternative ways of looking at or solving the problem.

- Change the subject. Look for a way to naturally move to a different topic.

- Suggest meeting outside work to talk about the problem. Be clear about wanting to do work while at the workplace.

- Mention places to get help, if you can. Suggest joining a support group or going to a treatment center.

- Be clear about your limits. Don't hesitate to end a conversation, if you're uncomfortable with the topic.

Using Computers and Phones for Personal Business

Some employees cross the line between their work and personal lives in another way. These employees use their work computers to surf the Internet. They might be shopping, making dinner reservations, or even looking for another job. Some employees also use their business e-mail for personal communication with friends.

Other employees use the office phone for personal reasons. They talk at length about things that have nothing to do with work. And even worse, some employees make long distance calls from their office phones. They may even ask co-workers to lie for them so they can avoid certain business calls.

All of these behaviors take advantage of the employer. The computer, telephone, and other equipment your employer provides are meant for work. So is the time your employer pays you for.

It's OK to give your work phone number to your family. Of course, they should be able to reach you if there's an emergency. But it's not OK to use your company phone like it's your personal phone.

Making Personal Calls at Work

You should make appointments and other personal calls during your breaks and mealtimes. And make these calls from your work phone only if absolutely necessary. It's better to make personal calls from your cell phone or a pay phone. That way, you will have some privacy, and you won't bother your co-workers.

If you use your cell phone during the workday, put it away when you're done with the call. Don't set your phone to "vibrate" or "silent" and then check your calls all day long. Likewise, don't constantly check your phone for text messages and e-mails. If you're paying attention to your phone, you're not giving your full attention to your work.

[FACT]

Top-10 Ways Employees Waste Time

1. Surfing the Internet for personal use (45%)
2. Talking with co-workers (23%)
3. Working on personal matters (7%)
4. Daydreaming (4%)
5. Leaving work to run errands (3%)
6. Making personal phone calls (2%)
7. Applying for other jobs (1%)
8. Planning personal events (1%)
9. Arriving late and leaving early (1%)
10. Other (13%)

CHAPTER **4**

Relationships with Co-Workers

When you enter the world of work, you'll meet many different kinds of people. Some of them will be like the people you've grown up with. Others will have habits, manners, or speech patterns that are unfamiliar to you.

Some of your co-workers may dress or look different from you. They may have different values and beliefs than you do. Even the foods they bring for lunch may seem strange to you. So, you may not know how to act around them.

Accepting People's Differences

First of all, it's important to respect others' differences. It's easy to make negative judgments about people and things we don't understand. It's also easy to "stick with your own kind," rather than try to get to know people who are different from you.

But differences don't have to be problems. Keep your eyes and ears open, and be willing to learn from others. Hopefully, what you learn will make you less *critical*.

And once you begin to understand people, you'll respect them more. In fact, it's a *good* thing that everyone isn't the same. If we were all alike, we'd live and work in a very boring world!

Critical
Pointing out problems or faults.

Diversity Training

Many employers are providing diversity training for their employees. The word *diversity* means "variety" or "a range of different things." Diversity training helps co-workers understand how they are alike and different in terms of culture. Diversity training has been compared to learning about another country before visiting there.

For companies of all sizes, diversity training has benefits both at home and around the world. At home, diversity training helps co-workers get along better, which improves their productivity. And on a larger scale, diversity training helps employers better compete in a global economy.

Facing Discrimination

Another challenge may be dealing with discrimination. *Discrimination* is unfair treatment based on differences such as race, religion, language, and gender (sex). Discrimination can be displayed in several ways. For instance, a co-worker who tells jokes that make fun of your religion is discriminating against you. So is a co-worker who makes negative comments about your culture or language.

If you're in a situation like this, ask the co-worker to stop the offensive behavior. If he or she doesn't stop, talk with your supervisor about the problem. You can also file a complaint about the co-worker's **disturbing** behavior.

[FACT]

Fighting Discrimination in the Workplace

The Equal Employment Opportunity Commission (EEOC) is an agency of the US government. The EEOC enforces laws that protect people from discrimination in the workplace. Discrimination can occur because of someone's race, color, religion, sex or gender, national origin, age, disability, or medical condition. In the United States, it is illegal for an employer to discriminate against a job applicant or employee. It is also illegal to discriminate against someone who complains about discrimination and perhaps files a charge against his or her employer.

Dealing with Difficult Personalities

You may simply dislike a certain co-worker because of his or her personality. In that case, just make it your goal to get along. Focus only on the work you do together. If you're polite, *considerate*, and focused on doing a good job, the other person will notice. You may even be surprised to find that your positive behavior is "catching." (And that will make the situation much easier!)

Finally, try to be aware of co-workers' special situations. Someone may have experienced a death in the family or be going through a divorce. Perhaps another is dealing with a seriously ill family member. In these cases, do what you can to make things easier for the co-worker. Don't neglect your own work, but try to be considerate with a co-worker who's struggling.

Considerate
Caring about other people's feelings and concerns.

10 Most Annoying Co-worker Habits

One in five workers reports being annoyed by a co-worker's bad habits. What bad habits are most commonly mentioned?

1. Blaming others for their own mistakes
2. Having their cell phones go off and playing a bad ring tone
3. Making nervous clicking and tapping noises
4. Talking too loudly
5. Eating smelly foods at their desks
6. Trying to impress the boss
7. Having body odor
8. Selling children's fundraising items at work
9. Constantly complaining and having a negative attitude
10. Being late for work

Word List

abilities
absenteeism
accomplishment
accuracy
aggressive
alternative
annoyed
annual
applicant
appointment
appropriate
approximately
arrangement
aspects
assignment
assistance
attitude
attracted
automatically

background
behavior
benchmarks
benefits

calculate
capabilities
casual
categories
challenge
charity
checklist
clarification
client
co-worker
comments
committed

communication
compete
competence
complaint
complicated
compliment
compromise
concentrate
conditions
confidence
conflict
confused
considerate
consistent
constantly
constructive
contact
continually
contribute
conversation
convince
cooperation
critical
criticism
culture
customer

deadline
debt
dedicated
deductions
defensive
deserve
desperate
detail
develop
disability

disapproval
discomfort
discrimination
disorganized
dissatisfaction
distracted
disturbing
diversity
dominate
donation
duplicate

eager
earnings
economy
efficient
embarrassed
emphasize
employee
enforce
enthusiasm
environment
estimate
evaluate
evaluation
expectations
explanation
exposed
express
extend

financial
fired
focus
formal
formatted
frequent

gender
genuinely
gestures
global
gossip
grievance
groomed
guidelines

handbook
harassment
helpless
hesitate
highlight

identical
ignore
image
impress
impression
inappropriate
inconvenienced
indicate
informal
initiative
injured
insist
install
intend
interfere
interpret
invalid
investigate
invisible

judgment

Word List

leadership
legitimate
limitations
loyalty

materials
measurable
membership
memorization

negative
neglect
negotiate

obvious
offend
offensive
option
organization
overall
overtime

panicking
participate
particular
patient
percentage
performance
permission
personality

policies
potential
precaution
priority
procedures
process
product
productive
professional
progress
project
promotion
prompt
protect
punctual

qualify
qualities

raise
react
reasonable
recreational
refer
regarding
reliable
replace
representative
request
resist

responsibilities
retirement
revealing
review
rewarding
role
routine

satisfaction
schedule
screen
seriously
settlement
shift
shipment
similar
situation
solution
specific
standard
statement
strict
strive
suitable
supervisor
support

tardiness
technology
temporary

tempting
thoroughly
thrill
transfer
trustworthy
typical

unfamiliar
unfortunately
unpredictable
unrealistic
unreliable
update

valid
valuable
variable
variety
verbal
volunteer

willingness
withheld
workable
workplace
workspace
worthwhile

Index

Index

Index